Becoming Light

Becoming Light

A 21ˢᵗ Century Retelling
of the Life of Nano Nagle
in Prose and Poetry

Barbara Ressler

Copyright © 2018 Barbara Ressler

All rights reserved. No part of this book may be used or reproduced by any means, graphic, electronic, or mechanical, including photocopying, recording, taping or by any information storage retrieval system without the written permission of the author except in the case of brief quotations embodied in critical articles and reviews.

Scripture quotations are from New Revised Standard Version Bible, copyright © 1989 National Council of the Churches of Christ in the United States of America. Used by permission. All rights reserved.

Archway Publishing books may be ordered through booksellers or by contacting:

Archway Publishing
1663 Liberty Drive
Bloomington, IN 47403
www.archwaypublishing.com
1 (888) 242-5904

Because of the dynamic nature of the Internet, any web addresses or links contained in this book may have changed since publication and may no longer be valid. The views expressed in this work are solely those of the author and do not necessarily reflect the views of the publisher, and the publisher hereby disclaims any responsibility for them.

Any people depicted in stock imagery provided by Getty Images are models, and such images are being used for illustrative purposes only. Certain stock imagery © Getty Images.

ISBN: 978-1-4808-6801-4 (sc)
ISBN: 978-1-4808-6800-7 (hc)
ISBN: 978-1-4808-6802-1 (e)

Library of Congress Control Number: 2018914111

Print information available on the last page.

Archway Publishing rev. date: 12/12/2018

Dedication

To women and men
past, present and future
who follow
the small still voice
to contribute light
for others—especially
the Sisters of the Presentation
of Dubuque, Iowa.

1 Kings 19:12

Acknowledgements

The process of creating this book has been *collaborative work*. Many others have helped in a variety of ways, infusing the process with kindness, collegiality and enjoyment.

Three "pillars" who have contributed greatly include Sister Joan Lickteig, PBVM, Sister Ann Jackson, PBVM and Sarah Blosch. All three offered deep wisdom around the text, insightful response for particular edits, encouragement and sometimes a push!

I'm grateful for the many Presentation sisters, associates, friends and students who read drafts at varying levels of craft and completion, assisting more than they realized. Heartfelt thanks!

I remain inspired by the flame that is Nano Nagle, thankful to the Union Sisters of the Presentation for their invitation to entertain retelling her soul's story and deeply indebted to the Sisters of the Presentation of Dubuque, Iowa who have enabled *Becoming Light's* publication.

Epigraph

"All the darkness in the world cannot extinguish the light of a single candle."

— Francis of Assisi

Author's Note

Years ago, I read *One Pace Beyond*, a novel of Nano Nagle's life written by Presentation, Sister Raphael Consedine. In 2014, Columba Press (Dublin) requested from the Union Presentation Sisters a more current historical narrative of the life of Nano Nagle to commemorate the occasion of Nano Nagle being made Venerable. In response, the Union Presentation Sisters, issued an invitation to Presentation Sisters and Associates worldwide to submit proposals for authoring such a text.

Wooed by Nano's story, as a Presentation Associate, I participated in this writing project. Eventually the field was narrowed to two writers. I planned to finish my telling of Nano's story, selected or not. Not. Over the next two years, I finished the draft, revised and rewrote in response to the suggestions of many generous readers: Dubuque Presentation sisters, associates, students and friends.

As a haiku poet, I value concision and precise diction, striving to say the most with the fewest words. An on-going challenge I encountered was the plethora of *detail inconsistencies* among various accounts/source materials. At times, I used one source, rather than another, because it appeared more plausible and/or "worked" artistically with my retelling.

I intentionally shift points-of-view and genre throughout the work (between 3rd person-omniscient and 1st person—Nano). Chapters include prose and poetic journal entries composed in free verse style. These journals, *consistently woven* into the work, are written *as if* by Nano and serve to deepen her characterization, reflect Nano's *inner* journey and unify the work.

This delivery technique and purposely keeping chapters short make the novel's pace quick—an important consideration for the contemporary reader and likely reflective of Nano's own step!

This is the tercentenary year of Nano Nagle's year of birth.

Happy 300th Birthday Nano!

Barbara Ressler

Author's Note

Years ago, I read *One Pace Beyond*, a novel of Nano Nagle's life written by Presentation, Sister Raphael Consedine. In 2014, Columba Press (Dublin) requested from the Union Presentation Sisters a more current historical narrative of the life of Nano Nagle to commemorate the occasion of Nano Nagle being made Venerable. In response, the Union Presentation Sisters, issued an invitation to Presentation Sisters and Associates worldwide to submit proposals for authoring such a text.

Wooed by Nano's story, as a Presentation Associate, I participated in this writing project. Eventually the field was narrowed to two writers. I planned to finish my telling of Nano's story, selected or not. Not. Over the next two years, I finished the draft, revised and rewrote in response to the suggestions of many generous readers: Dubuque Presentation sisters, associates, students and friends.

As a haiku poet, I value concision and precise diction, striving to say the most with the fewest words. An on-going challenge I encountered was the plethora of *detail inconsistencies* among various accounts/source materials. At times, I used one source, rather than another, because it appeared more plausible and/or "worked" artistically with my retelling.

I intentionally shift points-of-view and genre throughout the work (between 3rd person-omniscient and 1st person—Nano). Chapters include prose and poetic journal entries composed in free verse style. These journals, *consistently woven* into the work, are written *as if* by Nano and serve to deepen her characterization, reflect Nano's *inner* journey and unify the work.

This delivery technique and purposely keeping chapters short make the novel's pace quick—an important consideration for the contemporary reader and likely reflective of Nano's own step!

This is the tercentenary year of Nano Nagle's year of birth.

Happy 300th Birthday Nano!

Barbara Ressler

Chapter One
Autumn 1731

"It's settled then," Garret Nagle stated definitively.

He could always count on his brother Joseph's wise counsel and untiring assistance no matter the problem, personal or business. Joseph's legal skill guided not only Garret, but also bishops, landowners and extended family. These were perilous times for Catholics in Ireland. Since the late seventeenth century the grip of penal laws tightened their stranglehold. King William made it clear, "No person whatever of the popish religion shall publicly or in private houses teach school, instruct youth in learning . . ." What they had done through subjection to heavy fines, confiscation of property and periods of imprisonment was to deny Irish Catholics *any* opportunity. Continued lack of economic, political, social and educational opportunities would effectively reduce Irish Catholics to a serving class.

Every caution must be taken to ensure that the Irish not only continue to teach and learn in secret hedge schools, but also avail themselves, as able, to become educated on the continent. While education was personally desirable, for the good of Ireland it was imperative.

A branch of the Nagle family, merchants in Cork, had strong connections in France. Banned from opportunities on land, Irish Catholics turned to the sea. As "controllers of the wharf," Irish merchants such as the Nagles, with commerce contacts, enabled Garret to arrange with seeming ease a treasonous act. He would send his eldest daughter to France for an education.

"Garret, I will personally accompany her. Fortunately, our strong network of friends and our family provides us with options many others lack," Joseph assured.

Joseph's legal mind and actions were extolled by fellow patriots, though disdained by forces hoping to crush Irish Catholics and their faith under a heavy boot of oppression. Gentle in demeanor but strong in character, akin to Garret's own, Joseph's tall and commanding presence spoke.

"Joseph, we've faced many challenges together and with Providence we've prevailed," Garret noted, as if to convince himself as much as Joseph.

Joseph had "converted" to Protestantism in order to legally retain property on behalf of the Roman Catholic members of his family, as required under the penal laws. This way, the Nagles kept hold of extensive property at Ballygriffin and beyond.

It would not be easy to let Honora, their firstborn, go. Yet her father felt the risk to send her to France for an education was an investment, not only in Nano, *but also* in the future of Ireland. He took exceptional delight in watching Honora, "Nano" as he affectionately called her, frolic and blossom at Ballygriffin. She possessed her mother's beauty and although he didn't readily admit it, his own adventurous, high-spirited nature that often vexed his lovely wife. She strove to instill in Nano ladylike decorum and discipline. It could have been only yesterday that she giddily spurted out her disbelief, "Papa, is this *really* for me?" as he presented her with a little white pony and riding gear for her tenth birthday.

Nano knew the Nagle property by heart, having surveyed it often on horseback with her laughter and sparkle as constant companions. As she traversed the familiar hills and valleys, her imagination was stirred and her soul fed.

During family walks and rides around the Nagle grounds with Ann and their seven children (five girls and two boys), Garret pointed out specific flower and fauna enhancing the property. He shared his love for their land, Ireland, referring to it as "the landscape of home." He impressed upon Nano a deep, abiding appreciation for a sense of place and nature—the Nagle Mountains stood as witness. Simply looking out to the horizon at these mountains imbued one with courage.

With confidence in his brother, Joseph, who exemplified the family motto, "Not words, but deeds," Garret confirmed the plan upon which he and his wife, Ann, had agreed. After Christmas their eldest daughter, fourteen-year-old Nano, would sail with Uncle Joseph on a Bristol trading ship "smuggling" her to France where she could attend a convent boarding school.

Nano's parents took comfort knowing an extended network of relatives happily anticipated her arrival. There was cousin, Sir Richard Nagle, with whom Garret and Joseph maintained a particularly close relationship. The Nagles in Ireland had strong connections on the European Continent, both business and personal. In addition to Sir Richard, whose father had set up a Nagle home in Paris when his Irish lands were confiscated, there were numerous other cousins. A regular "Irish colony" grew in France where hundreds of Irish families lived, escaping the poverty and oppression imposed by the power grid of the Irish government on Irish Catholics.

The Secret

I can't tell anyone.
The Penal Laws
forbid education—
but journals don't talk.

Mother and Father
say arrangements
are in place.

After Christmas
I will travel with Uncle Joseph
to Paris, France.

The trip will be difficult
and I will need to behave
and be brave.

Father says
it's the only way
I can get a solid education.

Mother says
It will be only for a few years.
I will leave a girl
and return a lady.

We'll see.

Chapter Two
En Route To France

Dark. Wet. Cold.

Once on the ship, realizing that she would not see her family for a few years, Nano was nearly overcome with emotion. Uncle Joseph noticed. He quickly responded engaging her with talk of Paris. With firsthand knowledge he described the cafes, the grand boulevards, the art and architecture—noting the famous Cathedral of Notre Dame, high society and all manner of things Paris had to offer. Soon her eyes grew heavy and Joseph felt her slump, asleep at his side, her head nestled against his arm. He was grateful for her peace and calm.

Though Nano could be strong-willed and precocious, Joseph, like his brother, Garret, also detected the promise of her virtues and the groundedness of her being. He took comfort in the fact that Nano viewed the voyage as an adventure. He, on the other hand, realized it was a treasonous trip, a grave crime. God willing, they would one day recount it with pleasure.

Honora Nagle didn't need to open her eyes to realize that her surroundings were bleak. While she was aware they would travel by way of a cargo vessel rather than a passenger ship, she had imagined a more comfortable setting. "I didn't know it would take so long," Nano said.

"Nano." The voice was soft, yet firm. Her favorite uncle stood over her. "Please, try not to complain. Your mother and father are sacrificing to send you to France." She knew that, and she was grateful. Since the English rule had shifted to one of Irish Catholic persecution, Ireland and the Nagle family had been on edge. They couldn't openly practice their faith or attend school. Restrictions rested uneasily with Nano as did the confinement of the ship. She shifted in her seat and settled back into reading.

Nano and Uncle Joseph sat with a sprinkling of other passengers. The ship rocked harshly traveling in the turbulent waters. Nano stirred again. Joseph warmly patted her shoulder. "I just need to stretch," she said. Nano slowly stood up drying clammy hands on her skirt. Joseph looked at his niece, his warm blue eyes wide in the flickering light from a single nearby lantern.

"Nano, I appreciate your patience; the trip has required much from you and you have confirmed the confidence your father has placed in you."

"Thank you, Uncle Joseph. Have you heard lately how much longer before we'll arrive?"

"I'll inquire. We are getting close. Stay here. The sea is rough," her uncle cautioned. Returning he made his way from a wooden ladder leading to an upper deck. "Above deck it's a little brighter," Joseph encouraged. "I caught the sound of men shouting 'Land!' overhead."

Following her uncle, amid the bustle of passengers eager to disembark, Nano squinted through the gray. A dark mass loomed before them: France. "We've made it to France!"

Teasingly, he ruffled Nano's hair, "Just making you presentable!"

"Can you believe we made it?" Nano joyfully wrapped her arms around him. For a moment he held Garret's treasure tightly.

"And that means you'll be able to attend school," he reminded her. Nano imagined Parisian life: the fun, the gowns, parties, the food . . . . "Nano," Joseph reminded, "You're here for an education. Your mother and father were clear that's to come first."

"I know," Nano said, sheepishly. She brushed her hair out of her eyes. "Well, I suppose it's a good thing," she mused. "I haven't dresses for fancy parties anyway.

France, 1731

I will miss Ballygriffin,
the lush Blackwater Valley,
the backdrop of our Nagle Mountains,
so large and looming—beautiful.

I even miss Mr. O'Halloran's hedge school lessons
covertly delivered in the ruins of Monanimy Castle.
Did I actually write that?
Everyone knows my attention
was constantly being pulled
by the lure of adventure,
horseback riding,
climbing the magnificent ash tree,
(Father says it's one-hundred-years-old.)

I miss outsmarting the sheep,
stepping up and over their rock wall confines.
I will also miss
fishing for trout in the River Blackwater
with David and Joseph.
I won't miss worms.

What I love about Ballygriffin
is everything.
Mother and Father,
David, Mary, Ann, Joseph,
(and the two little girls)
Catherine and Elizabeth.

Everything.

Chapter Three
A Nagle Welcome

Many Nagle relatives, Irish nobles and gentlemen, resided in Paris, some at the Palace of St. Germaine's having followed King James II into exile at the invitation of King Louis the XIV.

Upon arrival Joseph immediately spotted his cousin, Sir Richard Nagle. "Welcome to France, Joseph!" Sir Richard extended a hand. Turning with a smile, he glanced kindly at Nano suggesting, "This must be Garret's Nano. Welcome cousin." It was obvious that the painstaking plans for the voyage and arrangements for Nano's stay had been well orchestrated. A carriage and driver awaited them. Though travel-weary, Nano responded politely. The youthful driver's rugged good looks reminded her of a classmate at the hedge school, one of the look-out boys, whose task was to alert the hedge master to the presence of any hostile authorities, so all could scatter--especially the hedge master. He offered Nano a hand to assist her in entering the carriage.

"Let me help you, Miss Nagle." Uncle Joseph followed. They were off.

"Uncle Joseph, how will I ever learn French?" Nano implored.

"Don't worry, Nano. We all smile and laugh in the same language," he assured her. Patting her hand he added, "One conversation at a time." Teasing, Uncle Joseph winked, "Are you ready to practice your French, Nano? You could start with the driver."

The outdoor staircase to Sir Richard's residence caught Nano's attention. It formed a half circle in front of the doors. Nano's eyes widened. She whispered to Uncle Joseph, "Look, two staircases! Is one for entering and another for leaving? Which one do we take?"

There was no need to worry about which staircase to enter; Sir Richard led them up the stairs on the right and into the house. Once inside Richard's wife, Jane, and their seven sons and six beautiful daughters who had been anticipating Nano's arrival circled around her. "Welcome cousin Nano!" they chanted in unison.

Nano smiled in response. Suddenly aware that tears were running down her cheeks, she emitted a giggle. They giggled. There were giggles all around—Nano, the girls: Mary, Brigid, Anne, Ellen, Helen and little Nellie; then, the boys, too. Uncle Joseph was reassured that Nano would learn French. In fact, she had already begun with friendship and fun. Nano had a liveliness and loveliness that endeared her to others. He would happily replay this scene to Nano's family upon his return to Ireland.

We Made It

The voyage: Water, water, water
and more water—storms
with driving rains!
Finally we made land—
France,
we're here!

Just as back in Ballygriffin,
when David and I
tricked the sheep
by stepping over the field's rock walls,
Uncle Joseph and I
'gave the slip'
to Ireland's Penal Laws.

At Sir Richard's residence
more water—my own this time
tears of relief, joy and sadness
all mingled together
like me with my thirteen cousins
—new fast friends.
Adventure.
That's what this is.

Uncle Joseph taught me
my first French word:
amitié.
Friendship.

Chapter Four
The Convent School

Later that week Sir Richard took Nano and a few cousins to visit the convent school and enroll Nano. "I'm Sister Mary Ursula, Miss Nagle," said the serious but pleasant nun. "Ready to see the school?"

Nano nodded, "Yes Sister."

"This room will be your classroom," Sister Mary Ursula pointed out.

Such a contrast to the Irish hedge school! The classroom was indoors, warm, comfortable, secure with desks and books—such a luxury.

Showing Nano the chapel, Sister declared, "You will attend daily Mass." Nano remembered the infrequency with which she could attend Mass in Ireland. It was too dangerous to attend at the Mass Rock after dark. Her family risked it when they could, which was not as often as they wished.

As they entered the dormitory area, Sister placed her slender index finger to her lips. "Shhh, silence is observed in this area at all times for discipline's sake, study and sleep, too."

Nano leaned toward Bridgid whispering softly, "I hate silence." Cousin Brigid's eyes widened in delight at Nano's audacity. They both emitted a quick giggle. When Sister Mary Ursula looked their way, they immediately quieted.

The large dormitory room housed rows of neatly dressed beds encircled by curtains. Nano noticed only two small windows placed high in the wall. How would she be able to look out?

When the indoor tour ended, Nano felt almost palpable relief as they entered the schoolyard. Since leaving Ireland, including the covert travel experience, she had felt hemmed in. She knew she would miss her home—Ireland, specifically the wide, open spaces of Ballygriffin and the fields of the Blackwater Valley where she had spent her days cavorting, seeking fun and creating mischief. It was as if Nano had held her breath until then.

Before them lay a very small fenced-in area. Sister Ursula motioned to it. "This area is used for recreation, exercise and games," she informed.

Nano's heart sank. She knew things were about to change; it was beginning to feel less like adventure and more like confinement. She smiled, belying her unease and quickly offered a cordial "Thank you." Following the weekend at Cousin Nagle's home, Nano would return to the convent school to begin her formal education.

At times Nano thought of her mother's many admonitions. She missed her mother and for a moment understood her as never before. Though she couldn't send letters home through the postal service, when possible she did send letters of news and love to her family with visitors returning to Ireland. Yes, she *was* studying! She was also holding tightly to her faith. No, she had not lost her mother's parting gifts of a Penal cross and rosary—as her mother feared. In fact, the regimentation of the convent school gave her cause to use them often, coupled with the comfort they provided in times of homesickness.

Here and There: France and Ballygriffin

Lately, I find myself
engaging in a kind of game.
I call it "Here and There".
The contrasts play on me,
in me really.

Here and There

Confines of the city
Freedom of the Blackwater Valley

Small dormitory windows
Vista of our Nagle Mountains

Hemmed-in schoolyard
The vast Nagle hills

Keeping silence
The sounds of nature

France stretches me
Ireland grounds me.

Father was right
it is the landscape of home

I'm here
I'm there.

Chapter Five
Sharing Ireland

Six months after arriving in Paris, and with Uncle Joseph long-gone, Nano had acclimated to life in France. While she thought of home daily, the structure and routine of the convent school nurtured a self-discipline Nano failed to demonstrate in her younger years. Despite the seriousness of her purpose in France, she regularly found time for enjoyment.

Nano expressed her sense of play and joy through laughter, often at herself, as she tried out her less-than-fluent French—making typical mistakes that created mirth all around. Nano was a ready customer for amusement. And she found that laughing at her own expense drew some of the more reserved and sophisticated French girls into her outwardly rippling circle of friendship. "Nano, tell us another story of Ireland," classmates urged. It didn't take much. Recounting stories allowed her to visit Ireland for a brief respite, if only in her mind.

"I want to hear another ghost story, Nano, please?" still another classmate begged. Nano often set her stories in the ruins of Monanimy Castle, and also in the lush wooded areas along the beautiful River Blackwater. On long walks together Nano took delight in entertaining classmates with tales of her beloved Ireland, delivered using lively wit, complete with antics.

Nano's learning pleased her and she thought her parents would be proud, too. Yet, life in France wasn't all work and no play. She kept busy attending parties, balls and social outings with Sir Richard's well-connected family with whom she stayed on weekends and holidays. Her father, funding her generously, made certain that she lacked for nothing.

Convent Academy Studies

Languages: English, French, Italian
religion,
writing,
mathematics, geometry,
geography, history,
botany, science,
mythology,
flower and landscape painting,
vocal and instrumental music
dancing.

My favorite subjects?
My classmates.

Chapter Six
News of Trouble in Ireland, 1732

Urgently, Sister Mary Ursula directed Nano, "Please follow me." As they walked together she informed Nano, "Sir Richard Nagle and Cousin David Nagle are waiting in the parlor; they brought a letter from your mother." The news and tenor of its delivery caused Nano instant unease. She feared what the missive might contain. Sir Richard introduced cousin David Nagle with whom Ann Nagle had sent the letter. Nano smiled, hesitant to take the letter.

Turning to Sir Richard, she quietly requested, "Cousin Richard, please read it." Carefully, he related the letter's contents:

Calmly, Sir Richard scanned the letter and reported, "Your mother writes that your father and Uncle Joseph Nagle were accused by an unnamed informant of being chief conspirators in an alleged plot to overthrow the current Irish government. This information was laid before the government resulting in Charges of Treason. Please pray for them."

Sir Richard, in an effort to allay Nano's fears, confidently commented, "Your Uncle Joseph is a great lawyer, Nano. With our prayers and his skill, I'm sure he will prevail." Nano's thoughts drifted to her father and dear Uncle Joseph. During their visit, Sir Richard and David talked further about priests and bishops in hiding or fleeing to the Continent. "The faith survives, Nano, and your studying here is a testament to that," Sir Richard observed.

David chimed in, "Many have died for the faith, as would I should it be my privilege some day." Nano drank in their loyalty to family and faith, but found she was unable to utter a word.

Treason?

Uncle Joseph and Father
are Ireland to its very heart
and soul.

Treason and for what reason?
I can't pretend.
I am frightened for them.
I am frightened for Mother
and the whole family.

May Uncle Joseph
find a step in the
wall of this mess
to step out with Father.

He did so bringing me
here safely.
He must do it again.

Chapter Seven
Ann Comes to France

Word came six months after Ann Nagle's letter to Nano that Uncle Joseph, using clever legal tactics, proved their innocence in the treason case due to lack of evidence. Another visitor from Ballygriffin brought even more good news. Nano's father was planning a visit to France. Nano felt restless in eager anticipation of his arrival.

Toward the end of her studies at the convent school, word came from Ireland that Garret would not only be traveling to the continent but he would bring Nano's sister, Ann. Ann would also attend the convent school and study in France. Nano's anticipation doubled. Though she had made many friends and enjoyed an active social life in Paris, she often fought off loneliness, holding it at bay. While others detected only a vivacious and vigorous Irish lass, beneath her social veneer lay a serious and discerning spirit.

Sir Richard was pleased to participate in the reunion of the Garret's family members. Nano was grateful to Sir Richard, his wife and their brood of thirteen children for their generous hospitality. She remembered how impressed she had been by the half circle staircase to their home. It wasn't long before she understood how well it served the volume of family, friends, visitors and "strangers."

"Nano," Garret, called with his distinct gentleness. For a second time in this same home she felt the depth of emotion—wet on her face. Her father had aged slightly but his smile and eyes sparkled with the same love she had remembered.

"Nano!" echoed a more mature Ann. They hugged and kissed one another for a short, sweet moment that conveyed a long history of family love.

As they moved into one of the parlors, Sir Richard, placing his hand on Garret's shoulder quietly confided, "I was worried for you, Garret, with the Irish government concerns. Joseph's legal mind is a rare gift."

Garret concurred, "Joseph can always be relied upon."

Garret then enlisted Richard in further conversation about the Charter schools in Ireland, commenting how they were a ploy by the government to train Irish Catholic children in the Protestant religion, as well as to keep them subservient. Ann listened intently. This was not the first time she had heard her father talk of the Charter schools. Back home, Uncle Joseph and Garret often discussed their concerns about these schools. Though she had not entered into the conversations, the topic captivated her attention and troubled her to the core.

Changing the subject, Richard disclosed, "Nano has been a delight to us, Garret."

"We've missed her, Richard, but knew you would welcome her as family."

"She has grown into a young woman since her arrival, and the eyes of many a young man fall and rest on her." Richard confessed.

"Yes. She possesses her mother's beauty," responded Garret.

Seeing her father and sister lightened Nano's spirit. Though her father would return home soon, she took every opportunity to show him that money spent on her education was a wise investment. For his part, Garret marveled at how Paris had indeed made a lady out of Nano as his wife predicted. He also recalled his retort to her prophetic words:

"Yes, Ann, you're probably right; Paris may make Nano a lady, but Ireland will make her a saint."

Garret returned home eager to share how their firstborn, Nano, who so taxed her mother's patience, would make her swell with pride.

A Question about Pedagogy:
There, Here, There, Where

Hedge school in Ballygriffin
French convent school
Charter schools
and beyond

There

I learned to name my love
for faith and land
in an Irish hedge school
in the shadow of the ruins of
Monanimy Castle surrounded
by hills of beauty
dressed in green
and sacraments delivered
at Mass Rock

Here

In Paris the convent school
taught me
the beauty of self-discipline
subjects numerous,
culture and camaraderie
kinship and kindness

There

The charter schools
take the children by force
from family and faith
in hopes of erasing both
Leaving only
serving the noble class
an option

Where

Can education
liberate the heart,
and mind
and soul
for Ireland?

Chapter Eight
Paris with Ann

Nano's classmates found the contrast in personality between Nano and Ann surprising. Nano's extroversion, vivacity and personal charm drew many to her. Ann's introversion, dutiful and quiet nature, at first caused her classmates to think her aloof. In due time Ann's gentleness, social sensitivity, and service-minded nature gave them pause. Before long the Nagle sisters were likened to the two sides of a shiny gold piece, both included on invitations to social events ranging from masquerades to balls to theater and concerts.

One evening in the dormitory Ann briefly broke the rule of silence. She had been studying intensely, and Nano attributed her preoccupation of late with the demands of schoolwork. "Nano, outside the cafe I met a young Irish patriot. He declared, 'The Charter schools will be the ruin of Ireland.' *Why couldn't we* return to Ireland and secretly teach the Catholic children?"

Nano reflexively placed her index finger to her lips.

Responsible and dutiful, it was not in Ann's nature to disregard convent school rules. Nano knew this. And she also knew that Ann might be thinking of returning to Ireland.

Voices That Beckon

Shhh. Shhh.
I keep the silence
Ann breaks
But there is no
index finger
that can hush
her heart's allurement
and keep its concerns
from transmuting
mine.

Ann is Ireland.
A large piece of it for certain.
The soul of it!

She possesses Father's
and Uncle Joseph's
concern for justice
and the poor
and anyone in need.

She loves conversation
about the policies
that dispossess our Irish
brothers and sisters
searching for solutions.

She enjoys talking
to the young Irish men
whose eyes burn bright
and faces grow ruddy
with talk of reclaiming home.

Me,
well, I enjoy
the young Irish men
whose eyes burn bright
and sport ruddy handsome faces,
policies aside.

Chapter Nine
Dancing: A Consciousness Shift

Nano possessed numerous elegant and fashionable gowns that she delighted in sharing with friends and now with Ann. She took pleasure in the excited talk of what she and her friends might wear to which ball. Tonight Ann had agreed to attend. "Ann, aren't you ready yet?" Nano chided. "The carriage will be waiting. I'm eager for you to meet the officers and young lords." She added, "Dancing is exactly what you need to put a smile on your face."

"Haven't I been smiling? I'm almost ready."

"Good," Nano encouraged. "If your feet are like mine, they will love the minuet!"

With ease Nano mixed with the glittering circle of Parisians. It was clear to Ann that Nano's romantic and lively nature was further enhanced by the social life of Paris that she so enjoyed. In almost yo-yo fashion, Nano sprang into social conversation and dance only to return to draw her sister into the circle. Both Nano and Ann returned home late, exhausted, but for *different* reasons. Ann could see how much Nano was admired by high society. While Ann attended solely to appease Nano, the source of Ann's energy lay elsewhere.

Dancing

We were invited
to still another ball.
Paris is so beautiful.
I can't imagine life
without dancing
and music.
I think I was born for dancing.
When I am dancing,
I am dancing
and that's
what I so love about it.

Chapter Ten
Ireland in Paris

"Ann, we missed you at the café," Nano said.

"I'm sorry, I was visiting and before I noticed, it was too late," Ann admitted.

Soon Nano pieced together the cause of Ann's increasing absences from spontaneous social frivolity. Charity work! Ann was visiting the sick and poor, while Nano indulged in personal entertainment. "Ann, maybe I should go with you next time," Nano suggested half-heartedly.

"Only if that's what *you* want," Ann gently replied.

Following her own suggestion, Nano accompanied Ann in responding to the needs she had discovered in the streets of Paris. Nano noticed how the faces of people they visited—mostly ill, visibly brightened at the sight of Ann. Ann herself came alive as she shared, essence to essence, with the lonely and sick. For an instant, it dawned on Nano—the Parisian streets *were Ann's ballroom*. It was on these cobbles that her step quickened. Ann found more satisfaction using her allowance to purchase medicines, food and other necessities for those in need than in buying gowns, hair combs, fine materials or other luxuries. It was as if the oppression of Ireland and its people had stripped her of want, any want that is, except to do whatever she could to liberate the spirits of others. There was no reserve in Ann as she moved about *her* "Ireland" in Paris.

Paris with Ann

I am blessed that I have
the company of Ann, my friend and sister,
who brings out the best in me.
It is not that she says anything directly—
but I know for certain the steady diet of parties,
museums, theater, social duties and dances
are a chore for her.
Don't be mistaken.
She dances well—so light on her feet,
and suffers no lack of suitors!

Her studies, Ireland, faith
and the future of our faith in Ireland
are never far from her thoughts,
betrayed by her gently knitted brow.
They ride in the carriage of her mind
only behind her visits
to the Parisian sick or poor
or those fragile in hope.

It is the invitations of need,
not breed, that compel her.
Where does she get that inner grounding
that draws others as moths to her lamp?
I just wish I could be more like her—
Faith with feet.
I love her so!

Chapter Eleven
A Troubling Tableau

As they prepared for a very special ball to be held in the Court of King Louis XV, Nano primped before the vanity mirror. "Does my hair look presentable? Which comb looks the best?"

"You look more than presentable." Ann assured her, "Perhaps you might consider wearing armor, as the courtiers are sure to fight over dancing with Honora Nagle from Ireland!"

It pleased Nano that Ann, gowned and ready, was waiting on *her* to finish preparations for the ball. That small moment fled when out of nowhere, Ann entreated, "Nano, I'm more concerned than ever about the Charter schools. Another one of the Irish patriots talked with Cousin Richard about them. If they continue unopposed, they will steal our children, our faith, and the very future of Ireland without so much as a gunshot."

Ann's words may as well have been a cannonball fired through the room. Nano instantly hopped up off the vanity bench on which she was sitting. "Ann," was all Nano could muster in response.

Ann implored, "We could return to Ireland, Nano, and teach the children."

Flashing her sister an impish smile and hoping to lighten the conversation, Nano retorted, "Not dressed like this!"

Ann fell silent. She walked over to Nano and reaching out, gently tucked a wisp of her blond hair under the beautiful jeweled comb. "Thank you, Ann. I guess I missed that," Nano said quietly. She coaxed Ann to stand with her in front of the vanity mirror. Nano pronounced: "Honora and Ann Nagle of Ireland," mimicking the announcement of their arrival at court.

Nano's smile ignited her sister Ann's, but it did not alter the inner call that Ann heard. Contrarily, leaving Paris to return to Ireland to teach was not something Nano wanted to think about when all of Paris was opening up to her. Nano resolved to remain longer in Paris. She had learned to speak the language and delighted in the social and cultural richness of Paris. In fact, she was starting to think it impossible to live as happily elsewhere.

As Nano, Ann and others were returning from the ball in the early morning hours the carriage suddenly jolted. Ann gasped, grasping Nano's arm. The horses were startled. From the carriage window, Nano glimpsed a gathering of poor French peasants huddled together against the cold. They stood encircled in front of the yet unopened doors of St. Germaine's Church. Peeking out quietly through the carriage windows, Ann commented, "Nano, they're waiting to attend Mass."

A mere tableau. But a troubling one.

Here and There: Tableau

Here and There

The evening's frivolity
An early dawn carriage jolt

Dancing at court
Standing at the church doors

Dressing for court
Huddling for warmth

Revelry without care
Waiting for prayer

Chapter Twelve
Garret Nagle's Death, 1746

Father's Death

We received word today that Father died.
They may as well have written
that the Nagle Mountains had disappeared.
Father dead.
I will miss him— mountains.
Can Ireland exist without him? Can we? Can I?
We will make arrangements to return home at once.

Previous to the news of Garret Nagle's death, Nano had not conceived of leaving Paris and the carefree social life to which she had grown accustomed. Now, leaving Paris was like the dropping of a kerchief. Her father's death drove her to seek the horizon of Ireland. Ireland and her father had become synonymous. She would not completely be without him in Ireland, especially at Ballygriffin. Ann and she returned home.

The 318 acres of the Garret Nagle property stretched from Fermoy to Mallow in the Blackwater Valley of County Cork. The River Blackwater served as a boundary to the property's south. It was here that Garret and Ann Nagel had welcomed Nano, their firstborn daughter and here that their ancestors had lived for centuries. It was as if Ballygriffin were part of the fiber of their beings.

Yet, Nano's mother could not continue on at Ballygriffin without Garret. She took up residence in Dublin and it was there where Ann and Nano joined her. Nano's brother, David, stayed on in Ballygriffin with their sister, Catherine, managing the house.

In Dublin

Dublin.
What was Mother thinking?
No matter how far
we move from Ballygriffin

Father, the loss of him
will accompany us.

Chapter Thirteen
Dublin

The Dublin to which they returned was a city full of need. While there were places of great elegance and wealth, thousands of poor Catholics lived in appalling conditions. Immediately Ann immersed herself in visiting the sick and poor, providing food, doling out medicine, blankets and her ever-present warmth and compassion. At times, Nano accompanied Ann as she went about her charitable work, but Nano was always eager to return to the pleasant surroundings of home. Could Ann not "smell the poverty?" Nano could. And she felt disappointed in herself.

Walking home, Nano turned toward Ann and softly called her name, "Ann?" She didn't know what it was she wanted to say or ask. She merely sought the warmth and acceptance of Ann's attention in this liminal space. She was not ready to embrace the commitment to continually serve others. Escaping, she prattled, "I have decided to have a new gown made." She continued, "That length of green silk we brought from Paris will be just perfect if only I could find it. Do you know where it is? Theresa Mulally could work wonders with such a fine piece of silk." Ann knew Theresa Mulally, milliner and kindred spirit for both her skill with silk and her sensitive service to the poor.

Sheepishly, Ann confessed, "Nano, I sold it to buy clothes and food for the family we just visited. I'm sorry. I should have asked you before selling it. You don't mind, do you?" Nano was struck speechless.

Of course Ann sold it. And of course Nano did not really *need* a new gown. There was nothing to say. In Nano's silence—an insight.

Ann continued to do her charitable works with no fanfare—and more frequently. Nano accompanied her when she was available. While Nano was edified by Ann's example, she could not fully embrace her singularity of purpose.

A Bolt

I thought I needed a dress.
Instead I found the undressing
of my want
bumping up against
another's need.
A momentary insight
offered to me from Ann
and delivered with words of silk.

My sister Ann
is my living parable
of another way
of being in the world.

She stands in God's grace
following desires
sown in her heart
by a gladdened God.

Faith, her treasure,
brings great joy
though it comes at a cost.

Chapter Fourteen
Ann Nagle's Death

Nano continued to struggle with the reality of Ireland's poor as she periodically accompanied Ann. She also viewed first hand a reason for their hope—the open arms and open heart of her sister. She witnessed Ann's world-transforming vision that moved her to ever extend and expand her compassion to Dublin's need.

One evening Ann returned home earlier than usual. Exhausted and feverish, she retired to her room. The next morning Nano's mother awakened her. The alarming look on her mother's face made it immediately clear that something was terribly wrong. "Nano, Ann's fever has worsened considerably. Perhaps you should enlist Dr. Fitzpatrick."

"Yes, mother." Nano said. She hurried out the door eager to obtain help for Ann.

Returning with the doctor, Nano led him directly to Ann's room where her mother was sitting next to the bed. Ann weakly leaned up off the pillow and softly spoke, "Thank you, Dr. Fitzpatrick." Then, she turned slightly to catch Nano's eye. In a whisper she quietly entreated her to please deliver the promised food and medicine —to the very place from which she likely contracted the fever.

Without hesitation Nano assured Ann. Sensing the importance of Ann's request, Nano set about gathering the items and left Ann's side only at her urging. In Nano's absence, Ann slipped more deeply into the fever's grasp. Upon her return Nano inquired, "Mother, what did the doctor say?"

"Nano, Ann's gone," her mother whispered.

There had been no time to thank Ann, or offer apology or even profess her profound love and admiration. Nano hoped that Ann knew it all, though unspoken. Ann's illness and sudden death left Nano numb. In that "place of hold" she pondered many things, especially *the source* of Ann's example and her joy.

Journal for Ann

My dear Ann,
How you scattered possibility
as you went about
the streets in Paris
the lanes in Dublin,
everywhere.

Only the poet, Hafiz pens you
beautiful enough:

It Felt Love

How
Did the rose
Ever open its heart
And give to this world
All its
Beauty?
It felt the encouragement of light
Against its
Being,
Otherwise,
We all remain
Too
Frightened.
　　　　　—Hafiz

I wish that I could show you
I wish that I could show you
the astonishing
light of your
being.
　　　　　—Hafiz

Chapter Fifteen
Ballygriffin: Backward, Turn Backward

Following Ann's death, in Nano's grief she turned to the intimacy of Ballygriffin. She felt empty. At the same time everything brimmed with memories of childhood, her father and Ann. The hearth. The carriage house. The River Blackwater. The orchard. The ash tree. The oaks. The fields and gardens. Castle ruins. She knew they would not be the same as when she had left, not so much because they had changed but because she had.

On a cellular level she took in the scents and sounds of the family home—Ballygriffin. Her senses, her very soul, stood on tip-toe as the carriage moved up the lane and stopped at the front door of the family home. At first she had not felt them, but when she released herself from David's tight embrace, tears dampened her cheeks. Were they hers? David's? Likely both: a salute of sorts to the idyllic nature of their childhood, to

Father, and now to Ann. "Thank you, David, for inviting me," Nano gently whispered.

The hearth shone warmly in sharp contrast to the settings shaping the lives of the children she had encountered while accompanying Ann on her charitable rounds in Dublin. She saw Ballygriffin with new eyes. She understood the differing gifts her parents strove to bring to their child-rearing, both the loving constraint of her mother's discipline and the unbridled, loving acceptance of her father. They sprang from the same deep and holy center. Both played on her, shaping her in a dappled light, as sun filtered through tree leaves. Her spirit was nurtured here, basking in nature, the orchard and flower gardens—a kind of Eden no Penal Laws could touch. As children they had roamed and run freely among the hills, valleys, and fields, enchanted by the ruins of Monanimy Castle, where they learned and laughed amid the landmark which despite its rough state stood strong and commanding. She recalled hours as a child playing "Who is king?"

David's voice paused her thoughts. "Nano," he said, smiling and pointing to the sofa, "Remember how we all pushed to get our hands on father when he returned from business? You always won!"

With an inner urgency, Nano changed the subject, "David, did Ann ever mention teaching the children of Cork?" inquired Nano.

"Never!"

"In France, before father died, she suggested we both return to Ireland and teach the children. She was convinced the Charter schools would destroy Ireland's faith and future. I'm bothered that I'm not doing something for Ann—and the children."

"Nano, come to your senses," David sharply reasoned, "It's against the law! We barely survived father's ordeal. Teaching would put us all at risk!"

"You're right." Again changing the subject, she added, "I want to see Uncle Joseph soon. I promised him I would visit."

In subsequent days Nano visited several family friends. Talking with them and their servants she was alarmed at the extent to which superstition and ignorance governed them.

As she struggled, the Spirit pursued her. Even as a child, Garret Nagle had glimpsed the "something more" in his daughter. Nano was spirited, people-loving, adventure-seeking. Where these qualities would take her he hadn't known. What he did sense was that Nano's childhood spent steeped in the orchards and fields of fertile Blackwater Valley and wrapped in the family's fabric of faith was sure to produce a generous harvest. Nature had rooted the Nagle children. And like a sapling, something was stirring in Nano's roots.

Ballygriffin

*Tucked tranquilly
in Southern Ireland
between Fermoy and Mallow
a backdrop of Nagle Mountains*

*Within sight of the ruins of the Monanimy Castle
the River Blackwater
Blackwater Valley
The arms of a loving family
held her secure*

*Room to roam, discover, uncover
and play each day
Paradise on earth
and warmth of hearth and hearts at night*

*Strong and tall amid
golden cowslip, primrose, daffodils,
blue bells and fuchsia hedgerows
year by year Nano had grown...*

Chapter Sixteen
Tea with Uncle Joseph

Nano carried a lovely basket of Catherine's blueberry scones as she approached the entrance to Uncle Joseph's home. The door opened wide revealing her aging uncle with his ever-widening trademark smile. "Nano!" he exclaimed. "I've been anticipating your visit."

"Me, too, Uncle." Joseph arranged for a servant to set up tea in his study.

Leaning back in the chair behind his desk, he inquired, "How are you, Nano?"

Nano confided in Joseph. She missed her father. She missed Ann. Their deaths had left a void nothing filled. Previous to their deaths, she had not understood on a conscious level how vitalizing their presence had been.

"In losing your father and Ann, we lost great souls," Joseph agreed.

"Why is it some of us live and some of us die, Nano? It's a mystery. And we have only one choice in the face of it: to *be alive* ourselves."

"I'm returning to Paris but I haven't told Mother, David and the others."

"And why is that, Nano?"

"There hasn't been the right opportunity. I broached the topic of teaching poor children in Ireland with David and he emphatically opposed entertaining *any* thought of it. You know it was a cause close to Ann's heart."

Joseph nodded. "Yes, Ann's loss had been Ireland's. And what will you do in Paris?" Joseph inquired.

"I am joining the convent; if I can't teach our children, I can pray for them," she reasoned out loud.

Winking, he teased, "Nano, you aren't asking me to smuggle you to France again, are you?" They both laughed.

Here and There: Uncle Joseph

Here and There
Father's
younger
beloved brother

"The most disliked
by the Protestants
of any Catholic
in the Kingdom."

Wisest and most
staunch family
counselor

Insolently
triumphant
over the authorities

Chapter Seventeen
A Convent in France

Nano fully committed to entering religious life, never to return to Ireland. This new life continually challenged her. Daily demands. A focus on small matters. The restraint of obedience. In the back of her mind, this mature head-and-heart-strong woman questioned, "Had she made the right decision?" She could not shake thoughts of Ireland, the future of its faith and its children captured her imagination and possessed her dreams. The decision she thought would provide her solace—failed. Sleepless nights. Troubled days. Her energy waned.

Finally, the divide between her inner apostolic longings in a cloistered world of religious life drove Nano to seek the counsel of a spiritual director—a Jesuit priest to whom she poured out her heart. She talked of Ireland, of the scenes and the needs she had witnessed on visits to the needy she made with Ann in Dublin. Ann's death. Ann's example. He listened long. He listened heartfully to Nano, essence to essence.

Softly he illumined, "The spiritual journey is full of paradoxes. Sometimes we come to a place, be it physical or spiritual, whose task is to trouble us, to wake us up to possibility. You must return."

Nano began to suggest every reason why she should not, could not, would not. She did not want to hear his counsel—had she not closed that door in conversation with David at Ballygriffin? And now that same door flung wide open again. As Nano stood to leave, he offered, "The way will open, Nano. Grace comes when we welcome God's work and it's always worth the wait."

As if the challenge of leaving the French convent and returning to Ireland wasn't difficult enough, Nano received word of her mother's unexpected death. "Some way to open!" she thought directing anger toward the shocking news. While her decision to leave the French convent preceded the telegram, she had not yet finalized arrangements for the return trip. Nor had she informed her family of her decision.

She felt a momentary, liberating peace upon making her decision. That peace was clouded over by deep sorrow at the loss of her mother. She had accepted that joining the French convent meant surrendering the personal comfort and contact with family. It was a price she had paid. Now the tension of competing losses, her religious vocation and her dear mother's death weighed on her. She knew well that her return to Ireland would come at still another cost.

There were many matters to which she would have to attend. How will she explain her permanent return to her siblings? How could she help the children of Ireland?

Both self-aware and self-accepting as she turned her sights toward home, she found herself asking new questions. Acting on their answers would create her future in and for Ireland.

My Penal Cross

Returning home to Ireland
nothing
to give
except
my heart.
For the
little
ones.

Chapter Eighteen
Re-turning to Ireland

Upon returning to Ireland, Nano faced grief upon grief. There was the embarrassment of her "failed vocation," the deaths of her father, Ann and now her mother! Suddenly it occurred to her she was an orphan. When the boat arrived in Dublin David met her. His quiet seriousness felt awkwardly distant.

Nano understood that David held questions about her return, questions she dare not answer even had he dredged up the courage to ask. She had resolved to return to teach the poor children in Cork. She had no choice, even though the family would disapprove were they to know. Later, over dinner with her brothers David and Joseph, they talked of their travels. David spoke of his upcoming spring wedding and plans to continue living at Ballygriffin. Joseph, who resided with his wife Frances, on some family property in Cove Lane, Cork, offered Nano an invitation, "With mother gone, you can make your home with us in Cork."

David, hesitantly countered, "You can always live at Ballygriffin; that is your home you know."

Nano thanked them both. "I'd like to live in Cork, Joseph. You understand, don't you, David, why I can't return to Ballygriffin just yet?"

"Yes, I do understand, Nano."

Mourning upon mourning. Nano again focused on her father, recalling that his unwavering love and support of her could not be replaced. In his eyes Nano was destined for greatness, though the specific shape of this greatness was yet to be determined. When Nano's youthful antics vexed her mother, her father was quick to counter her concerns about Nano. He understood Nano found correction and direction confining. Garret confidently suggested that in time she would become not only a lady but also a saint! Her education in Paris had accomplished the former and now with feet firmly planted on the Irish sod, Nano would take the first step on an evolutionary journey that would transform her, her family, and the children she would teach. Even Ireland would be changed.

Turnings: Here to Where?

Father, Ann—
now Mother, too.

From France
to Ireland
From nun
to none

From daughter
to orphan
From Ballygriffin
to Cork

From festering questions
living—into answers

The warmth
of your arms,
your hearts
encircle me.
Energize me
for the children
for Ireland.

Chapter Nineteen
To the Edge in Ireland—Cork

Though uncertainty lay before her, not knowing an exact path, Nano felt an inexpressible freedom. Since returning to Ireland any fear or trepidation was replaced with a trust in some impending revelation for which she could not find words. Living this beautiful question she was energized. What she did know was that Uncle Joseph would understand, as always. Her step was light as she made her way to the door of his home.

Uncle Joseph's face proclaimed his happiness at seeing Nano. With him there was no embarrassment in her leaving the convent. Joseph recalled their last conversation. Over tea, as before, they easily picked up where they had left off—holding the conversation of life. Nano shared with Joseph the stiffness in her reunion with her brothers. "Don't feel any shame, Nano," Joseph affirmed. "Our pain, suffering and healing connect us with one another. Ireland has taught us that. Our destinies intertwine; we belong to one another. We cannot afford any separation."

Joseph's wise counsel had never failed to inspire her. "As far as David and Joseph are concerned, there will always be resistance when something deeper than plans designed by human forces are unfolding. God provides when human control fails. I've seen it time and again."

The more they shared, the brighter the future felt to her. In this comfort Nano recounted her pain in France and it's resolution at the hands of a wise Jesuit.

Joseph suggested, "Consider the fox. When hunted the fox will set a false path to delay the dogs. Perhaps that was your purpose in the French convent." Nano marveled at this uncle who himself had outfoxed the government authorities with seeming ease.

"Uncle Joseph, that's what *he* said," Nano reflected and then repeated the instruction of her spiritual director in France, "The way will open. Grace comes when we welcome God's work and it's always worth the wait."

"And what will that work be, Nano?"

"I plan to teach children in Cork, Uncle," she replied, "I haven't told the family, though I'm living with Joseph and Frances in Cove Lane and looking to rent a cottage for my first school."

"You can count on my support," Joseph asserted.

This was Nano's usual pattern with Uncle Joseph: She came to him heavy hearted and left encouraged and inspired. Uncle Joseph was pleased that Nano had found the purpose she sought and was gratified she could use her gifts to meet Ireland's need. As Nano was leaving, Uncle Joseph felt compelled to share a memory. It involved a conversation between her parents. "Nano, when you were fourteen, your mother wondered if Paris would make her "tomboy" a lady. Your father responded, "Yes, Paris will make her a lady, but Ireland will make her a saint." Uncle Joseph, tilting his head reflected, "Perhaps he knew."

Here and Here: Revelation

Here and Here
Why is it some of us live
and some of us die?

It's a mystery.
I have only one choice
in the face of it.

Being alive
in times full of madness
is not easy.

But I am here
and so are the children
of Cork

Chapter Twenty
Covert in Cork at Cove Lane, 1754

It was at Cove Lane where Nano's inner self became manifest—where her mission aligned with the needs of the world. Her "inside" made its redemptive way outside. A small dark cabin. Mud brick walls and floor. A garret with thatched roof. This humble dwelling housed the beginning of Nano's educational enterprise. Working in secret for several months in order not to raise the suspicion of the authorities, Nano, with the help of Rose, her hand-picked maid, assembled her first students numbering about thirty girls. She ultimately employed paid mistresses to teach reading, writing and arithmetic as well as sewing, mending and other domestic accomplishments. She reserved the task of teaching religion and preparation for the sacraments to herself.

"Nano, the children are here. Are you ready?" Rose inquired.

Nano entered the "cabin", a former bakery storefront. The calm and certainty of her calling had taken shape before her.

While she had rehearsed this moment in her mind time and again, she possessed little previous experience to prepare her for its actual incarnation. Terror took hold of her. She felt caught off guard by the ragged crowd of the unruly children. Their language, behavior, the smell of their clothing in the confines of the small space nearly overcame her. Somehow, the Spirit provided. Smiling, she recited the prayer with which they would begin each day. The adventure began. The chaos that had governed their lives before attending school with Miss Nagle and her assistant teachers was not easily converted into an educational environment.

Yet, the vulnerability, kindness, compassion and tenderness with which she taught Ireland's "least" provided her with dynamism. Incarnational energy charged her work. She had found her calling and her chapel. Education was the healing balm that would free minds and souls.

Admission

Today
I met my students.
In truth I had been so busy
making arrangements
in secret
so as to answer
my calling
that I had scarcely
prepared
for the actual moment.

When Rose called for me,
I believe the hair on my head
stood on end.
They could not have seen it
under my bonnet.

Perhaps they knew
I was paddling in unknown waters!
There were so many children in the cabin
there was no room for air.
I had imagined it differently.

Tomorrow
we will continue our study
their's of me
and mine of them
and ours of God.

God be with us.

Here and There

I am 36
They range in age from seven to 15

While I have enjoyed privilege
They've known only want

I have been nurtured and fed
They've suffered and starved

I've seen the world
they reflect its woes

We share
a desire for freedom
and Love connects us
on a plain invisible

In France
I was them—a foreigner

For them
I will become
a window
to see Ireland anew
Its true beauty
alive through faith

Imbue in them
a religious imagination
that casts out
all fear and superstition
leaving room
for only love.

Chapter Twenty-One
Presence

Since the deaths of her father, Ann, her mother and now her sister, Catherine, Nano had come to understand how God makes use of the weakest means to bring about the kindom. Each day she left the home of Joseph and Frances, walking to a chapel adjoining her rented space. To all except those directly involved, it appeared that she was merely continuing her personal devotions. In truth she was.

The concerns Nano raised about her ability to undertake the work Ann had suggested years earlier, and the terror she felt upon stepping into her first school on Cove Lane, were now non-existent. She felt no fear, as if she had entered a consciousness beyond such vulnerability to discover an intimacy with father, mother, sisters and brothers—all of Ireland really. God was sustaining her.

Each day as she entered the school, Ann was there. She *was* there.

Heart Exchange

Ann,
You were willing to listen
to the answer of Jesus
when you inquired,
"What do you want from me?"
With you may I do the same.

Chapter Twenty-Two
Joseph's Discovery

Upon returning one evening from her school, Nano was greeted at the steps by her brother Joseph, so full of mirth he seemed ready to burst. Kind, sensible, pleasant and affable, Joseph and his lovely, devoted wife, Frances were gifts Nano treasured daily.

"You won't believe what happened today!" he blurted. "A man approached our door asking that I intercede on his behalf, so his daughter might attend your school!" Incredulous to the core, Joseph let out a hearty laugh. For a moment Nano, enjoying his pleasure, was almost drawn into laughter herself. She composed herself, realizing his discovery would be no laughing matter.

Softly, she stammered, confessing, "Well, huh. I am . . . I am teaching some children in a cabin on Cove Lane, near the Mass House."

In disbelief Joseph exploded. His face grew red with anger and fear. "How can you risk your life and ours?" he fumed. "We will be ruined! You know the consequences of flouting the law. We are lucky to have a Mass House and your school risks it all! We could face forfeiture, fines and imprisonment. Oh, Nano! You must leave."

Nano loved her family deeply and understood Joseph's concerns. How could she tell Joseph that she, too, had reviewed the potential risks of following her call—time and again. While she desired to address the hurt her actions had caused Joseph; she also knew she had not acted on some shallow impulse.

"Joseph, I will go if that is what you really want."

Frances, who now stood beside Joseph, suggested, "I think we need to discuss this further, let's have some tea and calmly consider things."

As Nano returned to her room before tea she prayed that further conversation might free Joseph from an oppressive fear that enforced the Penal Laws more effectively than any other agent.

The confession of her teaching became a gateway to her evolving consciousness. The enterprise of education might involve, not only herself and the poor children of Cork, but others of means who, because of an oppressive history and out of fear, abdicated their ability to respond in new and creative ways to keep the faith vital.

Once at tea and free of deception, Nano felt the problem of her school would allow her to profess her deep allegiance to the call which brought her home from France. For both Nano and her family, a more courageous road lay ahead.

"So, Nano, tell us about your schools." Frances softly urged.

While Joseph sat quietly, his face was set firm. At any minute Nano expected his anger might erupt again.

Nano wasn't expecting the tears that dampened her cheeks as she told in a calm and steady voice of her restlessness and angst in France. She related how her confessor assisted her in discerning what she should do and where she should do it. The only means of explaining her actions were divulging the details of her sacred story. Both Joseph and Frances listened intently. She shared that consolation had been hers these last several months as, not without challenges, she set her foot upon the path she understood as *God's dream* for her.

Frances again was the first to speak. "Nano, it's not fair that you don't have a school for boys. My support will depend on having schools for boys as well as girls. *All* Irish children need education in the faith."

Joseph nodded quietly concurring. His eyes softened considerably; impishly he added, "I guess I can inform that fellow, that I intervened for him and his daughter can attend." A soft ripple of humor floated around the table. Nano would stay. They would support schools for both boys and girls.

Joseph added, "Nano, You must tell Uncle Joseph. He has the most to lose."

Nano assured him she was planning to visit Uncle Joseph directly.

No Longer In the Dark

Poor Joseph
from mirth to fury
Dear Frances
cool with composure.

Exposure of my storied work,
not mine exactly—
but the Spirit's
No joke:
Thee in me.

Joseph and Frances embody
how knowledge can change us
and truth can set us free!

The schools are growing;
in addition to teaching girls,
we'll teach boys!

Chapter Twenty-Three
Uncle Joseph

Uncle Joseph was gladdened to hear that the burden of keeping her work secret from family members had been lifted. Though he trusted in her strength and steadiness to surmount obstacles, he also understood the cross of such unease.

"Nano, I have fought the Penal Laws all my life, Uncle Joseph stated. "You are fighting them also. Every educated student is a victory. I have made the necessary legal arrangements to fight through you upon my death. Even when the authorities labor under the impression they're rid of me, I will have outwitted them again! Only this time the operative will be much prettier!" He chuckled to himself pleased with both his plan and the dear niece on whom it rested.

"Uncle Joseph your mind never stops! Let's not borrow sorrow. I don't want to imagine a time without you."

"Nano, it is time to imagine it. We both know."

Uncle Joseph's ingenuity and strong faith served as a well of wisdom for the Nagles and in particular for Nano. Whether she was crossing the ocean to France or returning to face an ocean of unknowns in Ireland, his words and deeds upheld her.

April 24, 1757. Uncle Joseph made another newspaper headline—this time it was his death.

"He must have sensed something at our last visit," Nano said to her brothers when they arrived in person to inform her of Uncle Joseph's passing.

Nano continued, "True to his word, he mentioned that he would outsmart the authorities who persecuted the Irish for so long by supporting my schools to educate and liberate Irish children from ignorance and superstition through careful legal arrangement."

"You know that we are here for you, too, Nano." Her brothers affirmed. "We are proud of you and your work."

"I have no choice; it's the only work I can and must do," Nano replied.

Uncle Joseph's Death April 24, 1757

Joseph, your words
support in times of need.
Now you endow my work,
meeting others' needs.

Your legacy still serves, in deed*
'Not words but deeds'
the family motto.

But you, Joseph,
model
the best of both—
indeed.

*a legal instrument.

Chapter Twenty-Four
Ministry—By Sight in Day and Lantern at Night

By the mid-1760's, Nano had established seven schools in Cork, five for girls and two for boys. She served as sole supervisor of her schools.

In addition to teaching each day, at night with lantern in hand, Nano visited the sick and those in need—hungry for food and friendship. There was no stopping her. She sought out the aged, the ill and the poor.

During the penal days the English ordered all street lamps darkened. While this may seem a minor concern, many met with accidental death by unsuspectedly stepping into unseen hazards. No manner of cold, rain or darkness kept Nano, with lantern in hand, from her heart's work near the North Gate Bridge.

Pike's Lane. Wisdom's Lane. Portney's Lane. Cockpit Lane. Vanlewin's Lane. Watergate Lane. Here both disease and suffering resided. There was not a garret or lane in Cork that she did not know or to which she did not go with healing and hope.

"Miss Nagle, you shouldn't have come in this cold rain," Mrs. O'Ryan gently chastised. "The soup you brought last time I enjoyed for two days."

"I have only a couple of biscuits tonight—and look! They're still dry, though it's raining hard," Nano teased.

Without Nano's regular visits many would have hungered and suffered alone. As Nano spent herself she was filled. She marveled at her journey to this juncture that seemed not to have taken years but an instant. Steady outreach was balanced by contemplation. Upon returning home at night she spent hours in prayer. Nano's devotion to the Sacred Heart reflected incarnational spirituality, allowing her to see God in others and all of creation.

Lady of the Lantern in the Winding Lanes

I teach by day
and reach out
to the suffering
by night.

It's no wonder then
that I've seen God
all day
in the school children,
a woman with a fever,
the man sick with grief,
the desperate and desolate!

The miracle
is of loaves and fish.
I bring only the remnants:
listening eyes and heart.

When seen with evolutionary eyes,
we are light for one another.

In all of Cork
garrets full of God.

Chapter Twenty-Five
Collaborating for Mission—
The Ursulines

Nano struggled as her schools grew and required the hiring of a number of additional paid teachers. As the lone supervisor (in addition to her teaching religion) she observed firsthand the need for more curriculum unity and teacher direction. In short, her mission required not only help; it required the *right kind* of help. In response she consulted with Father Francis Moylan.

"Father, as you know, we have shared a concern for educating Cork's poor children in the faith; I need trained teachers."

"Have you considered inviting the Ursulines?" Moylan asked. "They are educators and they are mission-minded as well."

Having been encouraged by Father Francis Moylan to establish an Ursuline Community in Cork and upon receiving

Uncle Joseph's estate settlement, Nano found herself affluent in circumstance and possibility.

Nano could fund bringing Ursulines to Cork. In a letter, explaining the needs of her schools, she implored some of the French Ursulines to consider an Irish mission. She promised to build a convent school. While the French Ursulines were unwilling to come to Ireland to teach, they consented to train Irish volunteers.

Nano poured herself and her inheritance from Uncle Joseph into a building for an Irish Ursuline Foundation. Additionally, it required she make two to three trips to Paris where four Irish girls, whom she recruited from her family and social network, were being trained for the Cork foundation. She spent nothing on herself, so compelled to insure her ministry of educating the poor was sustainable. After her sister Ann parted with the bolt of silk to provide for the needs of the poor, Nano was challenged to practice the discipline of self-sacrifice and giving. Following Ann's death she understood each act of self-giving as a way to honor Ann's life.

From Here to There for Here

I think of dear Ann often.
Time has not diminished
her hold on my heart.

How pleased she would be.
Four Irish women study in France
with the French Ursulines.
who have consented to train them
to teach in my Cork schools.

Anti-Catholic sentiments—ebb and flow
as authorities "look the other way"
enabling my work to increase.

Uncle Joseph's generous inheritance
funds this Cork foundation
—building them a convent.
on adjoining property
I acquired with surprising ease
—it had been Nagle property!

Yet, Ann taught me—
nothing is really ours,
not even ourselves!

Chapter Twenty-Six
The Ursuline Cork Foundation

May 9th, 1771 marked the arrival of the four Irish girls trained for the Cork Ursuline foundation: Eleanor Fitzsimons (Sister Angela), Margaret Nagle (Sister Joseph), Elizabeth Coppinger (Sister Augustine) and Mary Kavanagh (Sister Ursula). Nano spared no expense in the educational and religious preparation of the four Irish girls trained for the Cork Foundation or in the building of a convent-school.

At the sight of trained Irish teachers for Irish children, Nano said, "Welcome home, Sisters! I'm sure our students will share my joy. Unfortunately, your convent-school building is not quite finished. I have made arrangements for you to reside temporarily in my cottage."

"It's good to be home," Sister Angela replied. The others echoed in chorus.

Nano explained, "The obtaining of a superior continues to pose a challenge. Be assured that God will provide. I am so eager for you to see the schools and meet the children. Perhaps we can go out tomorrow."

The sisters exchanged bewildered glances. Didn't Nano know the Ursuline's rule of enclosure forbade them from ministering outside the cloister? In France they taught the children of the ruling class within the confines of their convent.

Nano, sensing their unease, responded, "Is something wrong? I'm so sorry the convent-school building isn't finished and we have yet to engage a superior."

The Ursuline's rule of enclosure restricted them from ministering in Nano's schools for the poor as she had envisioned. Her schools were located beyond convent walls. Further troubling was the Ursulines' interest pursued in offering education for the wealthy. In September the Ursulines took possession of the finished building.

The obtaining of a superior for the Ursulines was resolved when then *Bishop* Moylan intervened on their behalf and a superior was temporarily sent from France. Mother Margaret Kelly (from Dippe) would serve as a superior until the foundation was sufficiently established.

Nano prayed, "All that God sends is for the best."— a response not of resignation, but teeming with generative energy as her contemplation called her to visioning, thinking, and living differently. Through imagination and action she co-created with the Divine and with others.

In spite of personal loss of invested time and treasure, Nano continued to lovingly and financially support the Ursulines. This witnessed her abiding humility and her capacity to let something emerge and not control it. Nano's higher level of consciousness was manifest in her trust in Divine Providence.

Higher Calling: Here and There
Nano and the Four Irish Women

The four young Irish women,
Ursulines
share my story.
Like me they came from wealthy families
and they offer their lives in service.
They follow the path
of their own
listening journey.

It is not my place
to alter the sacred call they hear.
I must follow my call
its place and pace—
beyond enclosure.

Chapter Twenty-Seven
Seeking a Means: Founding An Order

Though independent in her work and living, Nano had grown close to the Ursulines. She enjoyed their friendship. On many occasions they entreated her to join them, even going so far as to move Nano's bed into their convent when she was away.

Nano greeted Mother Margaret at the Ursuline convent with a smile. "I've come in search of something misplaced."

Mother Margaret's impish eyes sparkled at Nano's playful humor. "Then you'll stay?" she hopefully inquired.

"Mother Margaret, you and all of Cork know I can't. Mr. O'Leary's cat would not even hear of it! Ah, but a cup of hot tea would be a welcome pleasure before moving the bed back to the cottage."

Left with fewer financial resources for the growing demands of her schools, and beginning to fear for their future sustainability, Nano resolved to found a group of like-minded women to secure service into the future for the educational needs of Cork's poorest. Additionally, she desired that they visit the sick and elderly, and tend to the needs of widows and orphans. Nano approached Bishop Moylan with her new plan.

"Good Morning, Bishop," Nano greeted.

"Good Morning, Miss Nagle," he replied. "What brings you here this morning?"

"As you know, the dear Ursulines, with their rule of enclosure, are not of any help in my schools. I hope to gather some interested young women to form a little society to staff the schools into the future and tend to other needs of the poor as well."

"Really? Have you considered how the Ursulines will take this?"

"It doesn't really affect them. They teach within their enclosure. My seven schools for the poor lie beyond it."

"Yes, and we've been fortunate, the political authorities have looked the other way," Moylan asserted. "You know church authorities recognize only the monastic form of religious life with solemn vows and enclosure.

Nano replied with conviction and clarity. "We both know that the monastic form can not and does not find its way into the winding lanes and garrets full of need. A new form is necessary."

Moylan had continually found Nano to be a woman of courage and vision, willing to engage the question, "Where is God leading?" and always responding with the needed imagination and creativity demanded by the times.

"Nano, I don't think it's a good idea right now. It might provoke a Protestant backlash," the bishop suggested.

"If you don't want my schools in Cork, then I will go elsewhere," Nano stated.

"Well, Miss Nagle, I can see there is no changing your mind. I trust you are led by the Spirit as you have won the hearts of many in Cork. I'll not stand in your way."

"Thank you. It's not for myself I care, it's for the poor," Nano explained.

"I know. I have seen it. Go with my blessing."

Enough for Everyone

The Ursulines expressed concern
to Bishop Moylan
regarding the establishing
of a little band
to insure
schools for the poor
continue . . .

They educate
within their cloister

I meet needs
which lie outside it.

I don't love them any less
and "Now is the acceptable time."

While I'm able
I must put in place
a little group to carry on.

Much ado about my doing!

Chapter Twenty-Eight
Christmas Eve

During 1774, Nano took steps to sustain meeting the needs of Cork's poor beyond her personal ability to do so. She invited a number of young women to assist her with her work in the schools, visiting the sick and others in need. Of those who helped in her schools, Nano invited Miss Elizabeth Burke and Miss Mary Fouhy (who shared her vision of education) to live with her on Cove Lane. In December, Mary Ann Collins joined them. Directing their teaching Nano encouraged her companions, "Use ease, simplicity of words and affection in addressing the young." Encouraging them further she suggested, "Employ ingenuity in blending amusement and instruction." Nano was concerned that the students learn some practical and fine arts in addition to core subjects.

On December 24, Christmas Eve of 1775, the four became *The Sisters of the Sacred Heart of Jesus.*

"Mary, Elizabeth and Mary Ann," Nano inquired, "have you considered what names you will choose? I'm settled on St. John of God whose example of care for the 'sick poor' inspires me. I identify with the turns his life's journey took." Still undecided, both Mary and Elizabeth were silent.

Mary Ann said, "I find St. Angela Merici's story compelling. I select Sr. Angela."

The four received their religious habit on June 24, 1776 and Nano felt assured this new establishment—a mustard seed of women dedicated to the continuity of work for the poor-in-need would grow. Begun in 1775 the constuction of a new convent for the little band, in close proximity to her cottage, was still in process. In September of 1776 Nano changed the name of her foundation to The Sisters of Charitable Instruction of the Sacred Heart of Jesus.

Daily contemplation grounded Nano. Her central devotion to the Sacred Heart provided sanctuary to which she could retreat, find focus and be restored. For Nano, it was not enough to learn *about* Jesus. With each pace and at each place of her spiritual journey she was transformed by the cooperative adventure that ensued with every yes to God's promptings.

With Emmaus eyes she happily embraced her ministry. She felt one with the Christ who compelled—unitive consciousness.

The work in which she immersed herself and to which she invited others was ever-expanding.

On June 24, 1777 the four made religious profession.

Then and Now

From June 23, 1776 to June 24, 1776
What a difference today makes.
I became Sister St. John of God
Mary Fouhy became Sister Joseph
Elizabeth Burke became Sister Augustine
Mary Ann Collins became Sister Angela
We're still the same—
yet more—
synergistic together
for others.

Chapter Twenty-Nine
Seeking Means: Begging for Mission

Nano's evolution from socialite to beggar took place one pace at a time. Relationships transformed her. Loving and losing her models of faith—in her father, mother, sisters and Uncle Joseph strengthened her own inner call to deep unfolding. Contemplation and ministry, lived *inside out*, had transformed Nano into a person of welcome, wonder and witness—at odds with the frivolity of social circles. She was no longer enchanted by or engaged in a superficial social life. Rather her unlearning resulted in her living from "the great deep." As a servant and disciple of an all-loving God, she knew what it meant to be both blessed and broken. Happy in her schools, her surplus funds depleted, Nano turned to begging for the needs of those she served.

One day on Shandon Street Nano stepped into a shop whose owner was an acquaintance and supporter of her schools. She was greeted brusquely by the storeowner's assistant, "What do you need?" Nano asked to speak with the shop's owner.

The assistant retorted, "The owner went out and will not be back anytime soon."

"Thank you. I'll wait," Nano gently replied. She quietly exited the shop and sat on the bench outside.

Sometime later, through an open window she overheard the assistant conferring with the shop owner who had returned by way of a back entrance. "Was anyone looking for me?" he inquired.

"Some beggar woman has been waiting the better part of the afternoon," replied his assistant. "I put her out."

"Has she gone?" the owner asked. Glancing out the shop's window he caught sight of Miss Nagle.

"That's Miss Nagle, she's a friend, not a beggar. That is unless you call her—*God's beggar*." Opening the shop door in welcome, he said, "Come in Miss Nagle, it's so good to see you." She left the shop with a generous contribution.

Nano was no stranger to insults. Exchanges with former social acquaintances might include references to her students as "beggar's brats" or even worse, wondering about what business she could possibly be conducting at night by lantern light in "those places." Still, she took nothing personally. A larger spiritual enterprise engaged her thoughts and will. She experienced more rebuffs than kindness, but kindness won.

While begging in Cork, Nano recognized a stately gentleman astride his horse as he tossed coins to her. "Thank you . . . Sir James?" she spontaneously responded.

Taken aback at the sight of Nano whom he had not recognized, he halted. Dismounting from his horse he removed his cocked hat and intently looked at her for a moment. Something about her was familiar; yet the current state of her appearance made him doubtful this could be Miss Nagle. She had called him by name and the voice . . .

"N-Nano?" he stammered.

Her smile confirmed any doubts. It *was* Miss Nagle. Instantaneously he felt happy and sad at the sight of her—happy as he remembered her from their Paris days and sad at the thought of circumstances which had led her to such poverty. Embarrassment at his shocked response to her appearance was pushed aside by his genuine care and interest in his friend.

"Nano, what has happened that causes you to beg?" Sir James inquired.

"I'm begging for the children in my schools here in Cork—I teach them the faith," Nano answered. "The need here in Cork is great and I do what little I'm able."

Sir James was moved by the example of the young Parisian debutante, Nano Nagle of Ireland, turned Gospel animator. Offering her a handful of silver coins for her schools, he mounted his horse, turned to Nano and offered parting words, "God bless you, Nano, the Nagles, and Ireland!"

Meeting Sir James: There and Here

In France at a ball
In Ireland on the street begging.

Then dressed in finery
Now in cloak and bonnet.

There socializing
among royalty,
here communing
with fragments of humanity.

How is it I am
so fortunate
to companion
those made
unfortunate?

Chapter Thirty
Christmas Dinner, 1777

Christmas: A New Foundation. They had to celebrate. "Let's invite fifty guests for dinner," Nano proposed.

Each of the four members envisioned a gathering somewhat different from the one Nano went on to describe. "We'll invite fifty of those most in need from the garrets and lanes of Cork."

"How will we accommodate that many? Mary Fouhy inquired.

"What will we serve?" Elizabeth asked.

Nano had already thought it through. While a lack of funds was preventing a timely finishing of the school, surely they could provide, prepare, and serve a simple meal for the hungry using the tables and benches in the new convent classrooms.

Meeting Sir James: There and Here

In France at a ball
In Ireland on the street begging.

Then dressed in finery
Now in cloak and bonnet.

There socializing
among royalty,
here communing
with fragments of humanity.

How is it I am
so fortunate
to companion
those made
unfortunate?

Chapter Thirty
Christmas Dinner, 1777

Christmas: A New Foundation. They had to celebrate. "Let's invite fifty guests for dinner," Nano proposed.

Each of the four members envisioned a gathering somewhat different from the one Nano went on to describe. "We'll invite fifty of those most in need from the garrets and lanes of Cork."

"How will we accommodate that many? Mary Fouhy inquired.

"What will we serve?" Elizabeth asked.

Nano had already thought it through. While a lack of funds was preventing a timely finishing of the school, surely they could provide, prepare, and serve a simple meal for the hungry using the tables and benches in the new convent classrooms.

Nano's companions understood her choice to celebrate in the manner she suggested. Hadn't they just read about there being no room in the inn for Mary and Joseph?

After serving the meal, and wishing the guests a Blessed Christmas, they sat down to share the meager remains. Looking around the table at her "little band" as she affectionately called them, Nano was heartened by the joy visible on their faces. Working hard together had gifted them all with an almost palpable sense of unity.

The little band became familiar figures throughout Cork. A dynamism of sorts surged among them as they taught and lived in community. They felt so alive, full of crackling energy. Attending Mass, receiving Eucharist, and personal prayer animated their spiritual lives and their work as they leaned into the living edge in Ireland.

Christ Birth

*From a piece of silk and self-forgetting —
swaddling the Prince of Peace with deep intentionality
From Magi presents becoming presence.
Our "little band"
secure not in life
but in creating life.
Pointing always
to the One
who abides
within
and beyond ourselves.*

Chapter Thirty-One
1778 Theresa Mulally, Friend Visits

Nano first became acquainted with Theresa Mulally when Theresa operated a milliner shop in Dublin near the location where Nano resided with her mother and her sister, Ann, after her father's death. Their relationship, however, was later fostered through Father Moylan who was aware of their common interests. He shared information with Theresa about Nano and her schools in Cork. He also encouraged Nano to correspond with Theresa. In 1774 Nano wrote Theresa sharing with her details of her plans to establish a society for sustaining her work.

Ten years older than Theresa, Nano had been operating schools successfully for nearly 12 years when Theresa began a Catholic school on Mary's Lane in Dublin in 1766. Both shared a passion for faith education of those made poor in Ireland.

In September of 1778, Theresa made her first recorded visit to Cork. She desired to meet Nano, accompany her in her work and discuss their shared concern—creating sustainable educational opportunities for poor Irish Catholics.

At six o'clock on the first morning of their arrival, Nano paid a visit to Theresa and her traveling companion at a lodging on Cove Lane. Following a rap on the door, Nano softly called, "Miss Mulally?"

Theresa opened the door to find a slight, elderly woman with a shabby silk cloak, over a solid dark cotton gown. She wore an old hat turned up. Her clothes were drenched as it was raining heavily. Yet, her eyes shone with energy.

"I'm Nano Nagle and you must be Theresa," she asserted.

"Please, come in out of the rain, Miss Nagle," Theresa insisted.

Nano stepped in only briefly to embrace Theresa.

"I will return at nine, at which time we can visit some of the schools," Nano said. Smiling she added, "I often think my schools will never bring me to heaven as I only take delight and pleasure in them."

By the time Nano returned, she had visited three of her seven schools. She looked forward to sharing her Cork ministry with Theresa.

Directing Theresa's attention to the new convent building, Nano explained, "I'm eager to show you our little convent's progress. I started the convent building program close to my cottage in the spring of 1775. When completely finished, it will be a simple two-story structure with a door opening onto Cove Lane. A walled-in garden area will provide space for flowers and vegetables." Theresa smiled approvingly. Nano Nagle's passion and energy were contagious.

Nano further noted, "While I feel obligated to respond to the various needs encountered throughout Cork, I must prefer the schools to all others. Through education youth learns to be of service."

Theresa nodded in understanding and agreement. Their shared intensity for service to the poor revealed through their correspondence, had formed a solid foundation for a deepening friendship.

In autumn of 1779 Theresa visited Cork again. Upon greeting Nano she expressed concern about the growing fragility of her friend's health. With tenderness, Theresa cautioned Nano, "Do allow yourself some time for rest. Your cough seems to have worsened since my last visit a year ago."

"The Almighty makes use of the weakest means to bring about His works." Nano said.

Nano confided her financial distress that prevented starting a foundation in Dublin as she had desired. Despite having to share these concerns, Nano was refreshed by the friendship of Theresa; her magnanimity energized Nano. In moments when Nano reflected on their shared work she was moved from any sense of separation to a consciousness of unity.

There and Here: Theresa and me

Born in 1728 on Pill Lane, Dublin
Born in 1718 in Ballygriffin,
Mallow, County Cork

She's in Dublin
I'm in Cork

She won the prize
in a state lottery

I won by lottery of birth

In 1766 she started a Catholic
school for girls
on Mary's Lane in Dublin

In 1754 I started a Catholic
school for girls
on Cove Lane in Cork

Father Mulcaile encouraged
Theresa to remain in Dublin
Father Moylan encouraged me to
remain in Cork

Theresa wondered
whether it was best to continue
her service for the poor
or to enter a religious community.

I weighed the same concerns.

Theresa desired to enlist a
religious community
to further her work of teaching
Dublin's poor.

I initiated The Sisters of the
Charitable Instruction
of the Sacred Heart

We share a zeal for education
and care for the poor

Whether here or there,
We walk one!

Chapter Thirty-Two
Moving Day: Summer of 1780

Although the convent was nearly completed at the end of 1777, and "the little band" held a celebratory Christmas dinner in the new space, the transfer of the community's simple furnishings and personal items was planned for June. Word of the *Gordon Riots* in London stirred concern in Ireland.

In a letter to Theresa Mulally, Nano rejoiced in Theresa's restoration to good health and then commented about the delay in moving: "Then when the disturbances broke out in London, I was afraid to venture, imagining the same contagious frenzy may break out here. So I waited till the times seemed quite peaceful, yet notwithstanding we stole like thieves. I got up before three in the morning and had all our beds taken down and sent to the house before anyone was up . . ."

On the eve of the feast of Our Lady of Mt. Carmel, July 15, 1780 surreptitiously in the wee hours of the morning, with the help of friends and students, Nano and her sisters moved into the new convent-school. It didn't take long as they had few possessions.

Nano's concern for the health of others contrasted greatly with her disinterest in caring for her own. When pressed during Theresa's visit to slow down and take better care of herself Nano replied, "It is not giving good example, not to go through as much as others."

Despite the fact that the tubercular hemorrhages that challenged her in earlier years had returned with increasing frequency and severity, Nano dismissed Theresa's urging, "I think the little labor I have, the Almighty has given me the health to go through with it."

"Lady become Lantern"

Privileged Nano,
Honora Nagle, Miss Nagle,
Beggar, and finally Sister St. John of God
drawing
from the deep well of Love
gave her wealth
her health
heart
soul
to be a living lantern
of learning, joy,
healing and hope.
Contemplative-in-action
transforming Cork
transforming herself—
into lantern light!

Chapter Thirty-Three
Vision For Mission

Despite the demands of her schools, her outreach to those sick, aged and dying and the challenge of growing a religious congregation, Nano established a home for aged and destitute women in 1783. Wherever and whenever need called loudly, she heard it, and with her companions she responded. They personally attended to the needs of the home's residents—furnishing the home with beds and furniture, providing food and clothing from their own funds. Additionally, they offered the residents spirit-lifting opportunities such as singing, praying, conversation and card games.

In 1782 Sister Augustine's health had begun to fail rapidly; her death was imminent. Death had become all too familiar a figure in Nano's life.

Nano's profound engagement with harsh realities of the world as she accompanied others was sustained by daily contemplation. Her prayer fostered resilience, dignity, integrity and offered nourishment, healing and meaning. Nano recalled a near-final conversation with dear Elizabeth Burke (Sister Augustine), "Nano, we have both sat by the sick beds of others offering solace. But it is different now."

Nano nodded. She assured her, "Your work on behalf of our little band will continue Elizabeth. We will see it in each heart moved to join us. Everything is connected."

Before Elizabeth's death in 1783, four additional women had joined them, echoing words that her sisters had heard Nano often profess, "The Almighty is all-sufficient, and will make up this loss to us."

Nano attended to the variety of suffering she encountered in Cork, engaging it fearlessly, spending herself in solidarity with those in need. Beyond the needs to which Nano had already responded, she thought perhaps the community could address the needs of women driven to degradation on the streets by providing a home to restore their dignity.

Illumination: Unitive Consciousness

Have you ever
seen lightning flash
instantaneously
here and then gone?
Leaving you to question—
Perhaps you hadn't seen it
or
perhaps it wasn't lightning.

But then the vein of it
certains in you.

You are sure.
No proof.
The instant of illumination
gone—but no spoof.

But the truth of it,
the truth of it
lingers
like a gloaming
and holds
past, present and future
all at once
in Love.

Chapter Thirty-Four
Light: The Landscape of Home
April Twenty-six, 1784

Early in April Nano's health began to deteriorate quickly. Still she pressed on each day as if everything depended upon her. On April 21 after a weak spell, she sought rest in the home of a friend when a severe hemorrhage seized her. Her friend urged, "Nano, abandon working in the schools today."

Resolutely Nano replied, "What a coward you are! I have a good mind to go to the schools and walk it off as I usually do." Then, she collapsed. When she stirred to consciousness, she consented to return to the convent.

Nano took pains not to alarm the others. She informed them a short rest would restore her. She was firm in directing the sisters not to inform the physician of her illness when he came to call, attending to another community member. Her thoughts turned to all of the work that remained undone.

The sisters gathered tenderly around her, asking what they might do for her. She was slipping through the thin veil toward familiar, radiant faces. Reaching with outstretched arms, Nano whispered to all present and those beyond, echoing the Letter of John, "Love one another as you have hitherto done. Spend yourselves for the poor."

Entering the Light she was home.

Home

Father, Ann, Mother,
Catherine,
Uncle Joseph
Elizabeth,
all those who had preceded her
were there.

Her heart nearly
burst with union

Home in everyone—
becoming Light.

Afterword
by Ann Jackson, PBVM

Now and again during conversations about ideas and their application to "the real world," Barb would suggest, "Jackson, let's write a book together." "Yes, let's," I'd respond.

So when the email announcement arrived in the spring of 2014: "Greetings and good wishes from Ballygriffin, ... It is about Nano, that we are writing to you. ... what we are looking for is a novel which would be engaging and inspiring for the reader ... to commemorate the occasion of Nano being made Venerable."

Smiling to myself, I quickly clicked *"Forward"* to Barb, long-time friend, Presentation Associate, Nano fan, and life-long learner with the simple suggestion, "Write THIS book!" Interestingly, the Ballygriffin "due date" for the proposal coincided with Barb's birthday.

While we didn't co-author it, I companioned Barb, along with others, as she completed a book proposal, created an outline and wrote the required 2,500 words of "any part of the story" to meet the June deadline. "All journeys have a secret destination of which the traveler is unaware," wrote Martin Buber. For Barb, delivering Nano's story to new readers in a new century propelled her on a path of delight and surprise. After one of many conversations about the text, I observed and commented, "Barb, this book is *writing you!*" Like Nano, drawing on the deep and formative relationship she shared with her sister, Ann, Nano embraced a path she may not otherwise have taken.

After reviewing the proposals, the Union sisters solicited more information to decide which book would be selected for publication. An additional 10,000 words was requested by December 31, 2014. Interestingly, as the Spirit would have it, Barb enjoyed a particularly long Christmas break in 2014. Inspired to share Nano's story, she spent the 16 days writing two-thirds of the book. Still, much unfinished work lay ahead.

At the end of March 2015, word came that Barb's retelling was one of two finalists considered publishable. In consultation with Columba Press (Dublin) the manuscript, *A Dream Unfolds* by Sister Noella Fox, Ph.D., PBVM was selected for publication. In her article "The Nano Challenge," Sister Noella wrote, "I congratulate all who took part in this challenge and hope those who did not win will have the opportunity to publish their work."

Barb's listening and writing journey directly and imaginatively delivers Nano's story in this simple, yet profound book. The poetic retelling of Nano's life epitomizes not only Nano's *Becoming Light*, but illuminates how we engender and elicit divine light in one another.

In *Ask the Beasts: Darwin and the God of Love*, theologian Elizabeth Johnson reflects, "By daring to evoke the suffering, the beauty, the defeats and victories of people who struggled before us, it nourishes our own wavering commitment to the present. By connecting us with their unfinished agenda, it sparks the idea that something more is still possible."

About the Author

Barbara Ressler, an award-winning high school English teacher, lifelong learner, former Haiku Society of America President, award-winning, published haiku poet, gardener, visionary thinker and problem-solver, currently lives in Dubuque, Iowa.